MY LIFE IN TRUTH

MY LIFE IN TRUTH

MY LIFE STORY, MY WAY.

DAVID T GILBERT

Order this book online at www.trafford.com
or email orders@trafford.com

Most Trafford titles are also available at major online book retailers.

Printed in the United States of America.

ISBN: 978-1-4669-4682-8 (sc)
ISBN: 978-1-4669-4681-1 (e)

Trafford rev. 07/06/2012

 www.trafford.com

North America & international
toll-free: 1 888 232 4444 (USA & Canada)
phone: 250 383 6864 ♦ fax: 812 355 4082

CONTENTS

INTRODUCTION TO MY LIFE IN TRUTH

THE STORY YOU are about to read actually happened, the places and characters are real, and many are still alive today, and this story is written in poetry. The reason that it was done in poetry is that it is about my salvation, how I came to know Jesus Christ as my Lord and Saviour, and the events that actually happened to bring that about, which was by all accounts a miracle of God.

In my Church, my recognised gifts are encouragement and helps, the latter being best known as works of service, and the main reason for having my life story published is to encourage others that they also have a story to tell, and there are times when that story needs to be told in order to encourage others also. We all have a story to tell, and that story is unique, no one else has a story quite like you do, but to be able to put your story down on paper and publish it as a book is something else. I spent many hours recollecting thoughts of my past life, and trying to remember bits and pieces of my past that I had forgotten about, but were essential in telling my story in an exact way.

But even in light of the above, never a day goes by where I don't give some thought to the events of my past and what happened during those past years, not to mention just how far I had come since surrendering to Christ. One thing I have discovered since publishing my first book, unless you are doing things for yourself due to a desire just to put your experiences in book form before your story slips into oblivion, save your money and your time, because it really is a lot of hard work, unless doors of opportunity magically open up and give you a chance in a lifetime to make it big in publishing.

I have included other poems as well, some of which have never been published before, but being a re-launch of the original first book, some things had to be modified and added to, as well as changed, in order to have the publishing of this issue as hassle free as possible.

Even though the poetry in this book is rather long, I found that it was necessary to accommodate the story as a whole, as it is about my life story, noting that some people have written entire books just on their life. I have attempted to make my story as brief as possible, without going into too much detail, which I felt would cause the reader to lose interest in the story and therefore they would miss the important theme of my story.

In any case, I trust that my story would not only encourage you, but would stir you to action in consideration of telling your story, and thereby being an encouragement and inspiration to others. May God bless all who read My Life In Truth,

David T. Gilbert.

AUTHOR'S NOTE

PLEASE TAKE NOTE that those poems contained within this book that express a point of view, or an opinion about life principles, should not be regarded as 'absolute truth', but should be interpreted as by the above, as a point of view or an opinion only.

I have been with the Lord now for the best part of 32 years, and what I have written about was due to what I have observed within a Church situation, or because of observance through the eyes of a Spirit filled, born again believer.

All of the work that I do is actually based on fact, or factual events, and is due to having preference to writing about those things that occurred in my life that are based on truth, or have been experienced by me first hand.

I believe very strongly that when the task that one puts one's hand to is based on fact and truth, then that work becomes an expression of the individuals character, and therefore comes with all the heart felt emotion that the individual has.

As for my opinion, or point of view on the work in question, these expressions are how I interpreted the situations and circumstances that I went through at that particular time, what I was thinking, and what I was going through emotionally, and spiritually. Everyone is entitled to an opinion, and all should be permitted to express that opinion in a peaceful, non violent way, without duress.

I have chosen to express my opinion through my poetry, in order to stir up peaceful, open debate, and therefore open up opportunities for salvation. and maybe bring people into an awareness that, we serve a God who has no wish, or desire, to see anyone go to a lost eternity.

God has given us a choice, in which He will not interfere with, but regardless of our final decision, He will respect that decision, and grant your desire, so choose wisely. God bless your choosing, regardless,

David T. Gilbert.

Written and Edited, 10/ 07/ 2011, by David T. Gilbert.

MY SALVATION STORY, BY DAVID T. GILBERT

Introduction

OF ALL THE challenges I have ever faced, 'Parkinson's Disease' has presented itself as the most challenging of all, and at times, it is almost impossible to enjoy life in a simple and normal way. When I do have a good day, I enjoy the moment while there is a moment to enjoy, but with this disease, no two days are exactly the same, as each day presents it's own challenges in a unique way, and with each day, one lives moment by moment.

So, when the Holy Spirit prompted me to sit down and write this poem, He also emphasized an urgency about it, as if time was extremely short, and the necessity and expedient nature of the situation was not to be taken casually. With this in mind, I chose to be obedient to His call and put pen to paper. I have always had a burning desire to tell my story, but I have never believed, up until now, that my story could be told in a simple, detailed and understandable way.

There were many barriers I had to break through, many 'skeletons' I had to deal with, many truths I had to face up to, many wounds that needed healing, and all too many tears of past regrets and mistakes where I caused the people I loved the most the greatest pain. There were times when activities of the past were so painful to recall that tears of bitterness, remorse and regret flowed all too easily. But despite the pain of the past, the direction and guidance of the Holy Spirit has been paramount in writing this poem, because I have come to realize that obedience to His voice causes things to just flow so very easy, so much easier than trying to work it out myself. At most times, things happened with split second timing and ran to a perfect plan, working out so beautifully that I still stand in total awe of His wisdom and timing, and it is due to this that I have found a deeper trust and faith in doing things His way, and not mine.

I have also learned that the 'skeletons' and 'ghosts' of the past are not to be feared, but as we face them head-on and trust in His enabling, we are able to stand before Him in total confidence, knowing that God is a God of compassion, mercy and grace.

But, why tell a story in poetry? I recall one era in my days of youth, during my High School years, that I discovered the romance of poetry, and I enjoyed writing poetry very much, as it suited me very well. But, since there was no one to encourage me, and due to lack of knowledge, the opportunity to be a serious poetry writer passed me by.

My desire for all who read my story is that you read it with an open heart and spiritual insight, that you may be blessed in abundance, and that you may be inspired and greatly encouraged to reach far beyond your own limitations and frailty, and tell your story also, and to be so bold as to tell the world, that JESUS is a God of mercy, compassion and grace by way of the story you have, and that there is still hope, but time is so short, so the urgency of the moment would far outweigh any fine sounding argument to tarry,

May God richly bless all who read 'My Salvation Story.'

David T. Gilbert.

ACKNOWLEDGEMENTS AND DEDICATION

THE PERSON THAT I am today is due to my association with people of great influence, faith, love, com-passion and, above all, the utmost integrity. These people have played a very vital and necessary part in the development of a proper attitude towards all people, proper conduct in regards to my walk with Christ and before every person I come into contact with, and being an example of the highest possible standard, and in doing so, I am able to be a fitting and capable influence on the next generation.

First, I would like to say a grateful thank you to my Lord and friend, the Holy Spirit, who has been so patient, tolerant, loving, and gracious to me in a consistent and continuous way, I know that Jesus lives, and I know that the Spirit is a real person, I know that He is with me 24/7, and He cares so much for me, even in and with the trivial things, as He has proven many countless times.

I would also like to thank my BessieMae for being such a strength and encouragement to me, she is indeed my joy and treasure, and I love her immensely. BessieMae also did much of the computer editing, for which I am forever in her debt.

There is also people like Ron and Margaret Ingliss, who were gracious enough to allow me to give my testimony for the first time in their church, some 23 or so years ago.

Also, Pastor Ian Zerna, who unknowingly allowed the Spirit to minister into my spirit through his preaching, and rebuild my shattered heart after a bad departure from another church.

Not to omit, Frank Zerna, who unwittingly displayed a true humble attitude before the Lord, and has proven himself over the years to be the greatest example of integrity I have ever known. I uphold this man with the highest regard and utmost respect, he truly is an example well worth following, and I consider him a 'spiritual Father'.

There is also Pastors Paul and Laureen Newsham, who have taught and greatly influenced me to love all people with the same love as Jesus. I have been very privileged and highly honoured to be serving under their leadership, my loyalty toward them is something I could never go back on, because to me, they are God's anointed.

And last, but not least, is a group of people I regard as totally AWESOME, and they are the Youth of Salt church and their CHAMPION leaders, Joshua and Sjhana Greenwood. These young people have been a tremendous joy to me, even at times when I have had a bad week and need an uplift, they always show me the deepest appreciation and highest respect, and respond very positively to any encouragement I give. I truly believe that these youth are our future Champions for Christ, it is such an awesome honour to be considered a worthy role model for them.

There have been many other people also, who have helped me to develop a proper and fitting attitude toward all, and to be regarded as an example of excellence, but time and room do not permit such a list, suffice as to say, we all have people who cross our path from time to time, leaving their mark with us so that we are able to pass on the positive things we have learned and help in our own small way to impart Godly principles and attitudes to the next generation of Champions. I trust you will enjoy and pray you will be blessed, as you read 'My Salvation Story'.

Thank You All,

David T. Gilbert.

MY SALVATION STORY, BY DAVID T. GILBERT

Compiled, written, edited and prayed over by David T. Gilbert.

Introduction

(1)   This is my story, about the life I once lived,
             Of how I found JESUS, and the grace to forgive,

(2)   My life could have been tragic, with an untimely death,
             I needed a Saviour, to sort out my mess.

(3)   My heart was so bitter, full of anger and strife,
             I caused so much trouble, to so many in life.

(4)   I lived for myself, being filled up with pride,
             Until the day JESUS, called me to His side.

(5)   To begin my long story, not to miss any part,
             I will tell it in truth, right from the start.

My Family History

(6)   My Dad was a sailor, he sailed the seven seas,
               He saw World War 2, and many casualties.

(7)   He never told stories, and his words were few,
               Very little was mentioned, about World War 2.

(8)   My Mum was a tomboy, from Norwood she came,
               She was young, free and proud, carrying the Moyle name.

(9)   My Grandfather loved me, I was his pride and joy,
               I was named after him, since I was a boy.

(10)   My Grandma rejoiced, 'He's a blessing from above'
               I was her very favourite, and she gave me her love.

My Early Childhood

(11)   I was the main reason, that my parents became one,
                I was the first to be born, of four healthy sons.

(12)   My sister came next, before my three brothers,
                I somehow seemed different, from all of the others.

(13)   I took my share of the strap, more than I should have taken,
                It seemed to me then, that I was somehow forsaken.

(14)   I ran away from home, I'd forgotten how many times,
                It was like an adventure, and I would walk for miles.

(15)   It was my only escape, from the turmoil at home,
                I would run from the madness, far and wide, I would roam.

(16)   I seemed to be trapped, I grew up with hate,
                And found it hard going, just to find a good mate.

(17)   I would trust not a soul, and spent hours alone,
                My life was most exciting, running away from home.

My Adolescent Years

(18)   My Dad moved from Woodville, to Largs by the sea,
            Life was so pleasant, back in 1963.

(19)   I soon learned bad habits, which upset my Dad,
            I learned about rebellion, and turned very bad.

(20)   I would learn many things, in my days by the sea,
            I learned about girls, and gangs, and me.

(21)   I held on to grudges, I just would not let go,
            My Grandma would remind me, 'you will reap what you sow'.

(22)   I had heard about Jesus, back in Sunday School,
            But I was too proud, to be anyone's fool.

(23)   I recall one time, when I was 12 years old,
            I had a dream about death, which made me feel cold.

(24)   I cried out to Jesus, with tears lining my face,
            'Please don't ever let me die, or perish without trace'.

(25)   I never quite realised, that God heard my prayer,
            Fifteen years later, He would answer my despair.

The Loss of Innocence

(26)   But life was too good, I was having much fun,
            Life was an adventure, so I followed the sun.

(27)   I was so full of beans, oh, how great I felt,
            I loved all the girls, and made their hearts melt.

(28)   I arrived in old Semaphore, by mid '65,
            Life was so exciting, the Carnival, the rides.

(29)   The air was electric, I was having so much fun,
            It was great to be free, and live life on the run.

(30)   The jetty was the place, where the gangs would all be,
            How awesome it was, to live by the sea.

(31)   I made very few friends, as independent I was,
            I pleased only myself, I became my own boss.

(32)   My energy was boundless, I was strong, free and proud,
            I was King of my world, yet just one of the crowd.

My Dad's Heartache

(33)   But, as I grew older, and the years passed me by,
            Things turned really sour, between my Dad and I.

(34)   I learned of 'hard drink', to his disgust,
            Revenge was on my mind, upset him, I must.

(35)   I thought of past years, how he would hurt Mum so,
            He thought, 'he's too young, he would never know.

(36)   But I was looking on, taking note in my mind,
            It was his time to lose, so I began to unwind.

(37)   I would try to hurt him, in any way I could,
            I recalled my pain and suffering, during my childhood.

(38)   I made it my mission, to cause him great pain,
            I showed I was stubborn, time and again.

(39)   I must have hurt my Dad greatly, I caused him much grief,
            By holding on to the past, I thought I'd find relief.

(40)   I never felt proud, about Dad anyway,
            He would dress like a hobo, the clown of the day.

Friendships lost

(41)   I hurt my friends also, I acted like a dope,
          I was consumed by my folly, without any hope.

(42)   I was 18 years old, when the '70's came,
          I became very spiteful, and this to my shame.

(43)   I always blamed others, for my foolish plight,
          It was never my fault, 'cause, 'I was always right'.

(44)   I would indulge in hard liquor, and unashamedly curse,
          I'd party all night, the mornings were worse.

(45)   I acted so foolishly, embarrassing my friends,
          My anger and folly, brought my life to it's end.

A Friendship Cut Short

(46)   The bond that I had with my Mum was so strong,
         I was more her friend, than I was her son.

(47)   She would tell me sad stories, of times passed by,
         Of how Dad would treat her, oh, how she would cry.

(48)   It made me so angry, to think he could be,
         So cold and uncaring, to my Mum and me.

(49)   As the '70's passed by, we formed a strong bond,
         I became Mum's best friend, because I was so strong.

(50)   The '70's were fun times, sunny days without end,
         I had no idea, I was about to lose my friend.

A Miracle Amid Confusion

(51)   All was quite well, until one sunny day,
        Some tragic news, would come our way.

(52)   My Mum had a cancer, 'Ovarian,' it was,
        She had four operations, 'till all was lost.

(53)   When she knew she was dying, her only request,
        Was to see her friend's wife, and be married at best.

(54)   I had no 'special' lady, in my life when Mum died,
        I had missed my best chance, to show her a bride.

(55)   But, God had a plan, a true miracle, indeed,
        My Lord was the answer, to my Mum's great need.

(56)   As she lay in that coffin, I looked at her face,
        I saw a strange glow, unique to this place.

(57)   A small voice within stated, 'she's not dead,'
        But, I had no understanding, of that voice in my head.

(58)   As a young girl, each Sunday, Mum served the LORD,
        But her marriage was hurtful, so she turned from His Word.

(59)   She was brought back to Jesus, as later I found,
        By the one I would marry, who would settle me down.

The Down Ward Spiral

(60)   My life took a nose dive, from that moment on,
          My life was in pieces, after starting so strong.

(61)   Things got really bad, between my Dad and I,
          We despised each other, never seeing eye to eye.

(62)   I hated him mostly, with wicked intent,
          Never fearing in the least, if to hell I was sent.

(63)   Like a man who is blind, I just could not see,
          What my hatred and arrogance were doing to me.

(64)   I blamed many others, for my troubles and woes,
          Never taking account, as the Proverb goes.

(65)   I had wasted my life, in so many ways,
          Not realizing my hatred, would shorten my days.

(66)   There were many temptations, for a life of sin,
            Sin is a cancer, that destroys from within,

(67)   I cared not who I slept with, to me, it would never matter,
            I was watching my life, being torn to a tatter.

(68)   I used to cry 'freedom', and I wore a brass bell,
            But my arrogance and folly, were leading me to hell.

(69)   I was a victim and prisoner, my very own fool,
            I became unreachable, yet playing it cool.

A Miracle Amid Turmoil

(70)   By the time just before I turned 27,
       I would have an encounter, which would turn me toward heaven.

(71)   I shacked up at Rosewater, known as the slums,
       I soon became known, as just one of the bums.

(72)   My life was a ruin, an unholy mess,
       I had nothing to live for, and I felt so depressed.

(73)   A strange chance meeting, would happen that day,
       That's when I first saw, my Bessiemae.

(74)   She appeared quite cool, but much more than that,
       There was a glow on her face, and my mind went back,

(75)   To the time I saw Mum laying in silence, so still,
       And the glow on her face, it gave me a chill.

(76)   BessieMae looked at peace, amid the turmoil,
       I knew in my heart, I had to know that girl.

A Journey Of Hope

(77)   Over the next four months, exchanging word for word,
         Her speech was the wisest, I had ever heard.

(78)   We would spend countless hours, just talking about life,
         She was so fascinating, my future wife.

(79)   Time and again, we would spend hours together,
         I had fallen in love, I wanted her forever.

(80)   I had no vehicle, so for miles, I would walk,
         Her wisdom impressed me, I just wanted to talk.

The Final Battle

(81)   As our friendship grew, we were at ease and warm,
           We were not quite aware, of an oncoming storm.

(82)   But up in heaven, the battle ran hot,
           There was war for my soul, believe it or not.

(83)   Like a feather in a windstorm, we were tossed to and fro,
           It was satan's lawless lot, but we were not to know.

(84)   I was torn four times, from the arms of my Bess,
           We could not understand, why this confusion and mess!

(85)   It was later I found, there was a war for me,
           But our thoughts were carnal, and we just could not see,

(86)   I felt so helpless, I was about to fall,
           But, Jesus would soon prove, who was Lord of all.

(87)   He had a plan, sealed at Calvary,
           Where all mankind, would bow their knee.

(88)   A plan of Salvation, like an open door,
           For all to enter, both rich or poor.

Reminiscing Before The Encounter

(89)   Then came the day, in late January,
            When my eyes finally were opened, and I could, at last, see.

(90)   Bessie prayed for me, on the night before,
            'Bring him back one of yours, or may I see him no more.'

(91)   The next day came, and I felt so strange,
            Something was different, like a timely change.

(92)   I felt like my time, had finally come.
            I was obsolete down here, I just did not belong.

(93)   The places I frequented, when I was a lad,
            Were just ghosts from the past, I felt very sad.

(94)   I reflected on good times, oh, how joyful I would be,
            Living life as I chose, now a faded memory.

(95)   My life seemed so tragic, as I could remember,
            I was saying goodbye, before my surrender.

(96)   At 3.30 that day, I was at Glanville Station,
            There was music to be heard, it broke my concentration.

(97)   So my friends and I, went on our way,
              We headed down the road, to top off a great day.

(98)   Each summer, the Councils would bring in three bands,
              One hour to each, as the deal officially stands.

(99)   They would play their rock music, and sing very loud,
              It was a day of excitement, as they brought in the crowds.

My Moment Of Truth

(100)   At 4 p.m., on that afternoon,

        The scene was set, for an encounter with doom.

(101)   I stood there with my friends, amongst the noisy throng,

        This was my moment of truth, my very last song.

(102)   I suddenly felt, as if I was inside a jar,

        My vision was clear, but my hearing seemed far.

(103)   I felt two things, I never felt before,

        A love and a peace, so strong and so pure.

(104)   I have searched for this love, for most of my days,

        It was a love that broke barriers, and filled me with praise,

(105)   The peace that I felt, calmed the storm within,

        I felt loved warts and all, I was freed from my sin.

(106)   Those great chains of bondage, that bound me so tight,

        Broke loose in an instant, I was free from my plight,

(107)   I felt my chest open, my soul soared like a dove,

        I saw a brilliant flash, it was Jesus from above,

(108)   He opened my eyes, I could not help but see,
           He walked into my life, He died, just for me.

(109)   The last thing I heard, was the voice of the Spirit,
           'Your kingdom or Mine', and He waited a minute.

(110)   I had a choice to make, on that very day,
           In which direction I would go, and the price I would pay.

(111)   I thought for a moment, what I had to lose,
           But it was never that hard, I knew what to choose.

A Victory And A Pleasant Surprise

(112)   I said 'goodbye Semaphore,' and went home to Bess,
         With Jesus by my side, I walked from my mess.

(113)   I jumped in my car, and headed for home,
         I was safe in His arms, no more would I roam.

(114)   My BessieMae came for me, she finally had enough,
         But, I could never really blame her, the battle was tough.

(115)   She came up to me, and met me face to face,
         Not knowing that Jesus, had saved me by grace.

(116)   She had it all planned, before that day,
         To say 'farewell Davo, I'm on my way.'

(117)   She opened her mouth, to complain and groan,
         Instead, she said 'David, it's time to come home'.

(118)   I suddenly reacted, at the sound of her voice,
         She stood there in shock, but the Angels rejoiced.

Surrender, At Last

(119)   I went home a citizen, of Heaven above,
        I was chosen by grace, now I am safe in His love.

(120)   I have given my life, to Jesus, my King,
        He is my Healer, He's my Everything.

(121)   He is always with me, I know that for sure,
        I have never known a love, so deep and so pure.

(122)   He renewed my heart, I could finally forgive,
        It's for Jesus Christ, that I now live.

(123)   He filled my life, with a purpose and plan,
        BessieMae could hardly believe, I was the same man.

(124)   Bessie and I were united, in 1980, it was,
        It's been thirty years now, and I still know who's boss.

(125)   On November 22, the day J. F. K. died,
        It was front page news, when America cried.

(126)   That's the day we were wed, it was our special day,
        We both said 'I Do', then joined in to pray.

Dealing With Past Pain

(127)   My life was so free, I forgave my dear Dad,
        My attitude radically changed, from the bitterness I had.

(128)   I knew I had to make amends with my past,
        I visited my Grandma, I wanted to act fast.

(129)   I told her what happened, she started to weep,
        Her prayers had been answered, now, she could finally sleep.

Reflecting On The Past

(130)   I have been in His service, for about 30 years,
        And I still give thought, and remember with tears.

(131)   I often reflect on the events of those days,
        I have much to regret, in a whole lot of ways.

(132)   I had lost all direction, I just could not see,
        How much I was bound, for a hot eternity.

(133)   At times, it is so painful, to remember those days,
        I had been such a fool, in so many bad ways.

(134)   I made my peace with my Dad, just before he died,
        I believe he's in Heaven, with Mum by his side.

(135)   I could not hate any more, Jesus changed my heart,
        I wanted to love, and make a new start.

A Faithful Servant

(136)   I started reading the Word, I learned how to pray,
            I started to serve Jesus, in a very faithful way.

(137)   I did all those jobs, no one else would do,
            I developed a servants heart, I was faithful and true.

(138)   I learned how to tithe, a principle from the Lord,
            As each week I tithe, I honour His Word.

(139)   I remain faithful in tithing, to this very day.
            I am blessed with an abundance, in every wonderful way.

A Challenge Of Faith

(140)   I have lived my life with integrity,
          But just before, I turned 53,

(141)   My doctor told me of a challenge ahead,
          You will be stricken for sure, but you won't wind up dead.

(142)   You have 'Parkinson's Disease, he said, with a sigh,
          I sat there in shock, and I wanted to cry.

(143)   From the day I first met Him, I remained faithful, indeed,
          I tried coming to terms, with my challenging need.

(144)   I sat down and thought, about how far I had come,
          Since the day I surrendered, to God's only Son.

A Choice To Fight On

(145)   I gave particular thought, to what I did best,
        I was a strength to the people, a cut above the rest.

(146)   I would also encourage, and spur people on,
        They gave Glory for me, to the Holy One.

(147)   I would shine for Jesus, reflecting His Glory,
        So I made a wise choice, to tell all my story.

(148)   I knew what I did best, I was determined to fight,
        I won't give in easy, I trust in His might.

My Declaration

(149)   Each day is a battle, the fight still goes on,
        But my God is faithful, so I'l trust in His Son.

(150)   I will continue to be, a Champion for sure,
        And encourage the people, with a love so pure.

(151)   I will watch my attitude, and my example, you bet,
        I won't go down easy, I'm not beaten yet.

(152)   While my friends still love me, and honour me so,
        I will never be defeated, I refuse to let go,

(153)   Of the promise He gave me, when He went to the cross,
        'By His stripes, you are healed,' yes, I know whose the BOSS.

(154)   So, be encouraged, be bold, tell the world your tale,
        When you yield to God's Spirit, you could never fail.

(155)   One day, I will be healed, and enter His Glory,
        I thank you for reading, 'My Salvation Story'

(156)   We have come to the end, all things finish, of course,
        You have enjoyed my story, now, how about yours?

David T. Gilbert.

This 'SALVATION STORY' was finally edited and completed by myself, David T. Gilbert, on Sunday, 28/11/2010.

It took 5 weeks of intense research, recalling and remembering of every possible important detail of my conversion to Salvation, in which, I would like to include also the following people for their reading and reviewing of this final draft of 'My Salvation Story'.

Joanne Matthews, adviser and assistant in helping to have this book published.

Helen & Jessica Power
Rory & Nikki Zilm & their children
Simon Abbott & Family
Maria Woodland
Ron & Margaret Ingliss Story critics
Brian & Vikki Wheeldon & Cohen
Leanne Rehn
Daryl Ingliss
Ps. Paul & Laureen Newsham

Final Draft. 28/11/2010. Re-edited and updated, 8/ 8/ 2011.

BEFORE I EVER KNEW YOU

Before I ever knew You,
my life was in Your plan,
While I was still weighed down with sin,
You were waiting for my hand.

I was living life in my own way,
thinking I was just so cool,
Not realising that my selfish pride,
Would make me look the fool.

My eyes were spiritually blinded,
I was bound with anchor chains,
I put the blame on others,
Inflicting so much pain.

I don't know what You saw in me,
The day You entered my life,
I am so unworthy of Your grace,
I am always causing strife.

But you still went to that cross for me,
Even though I was bound by sin,
You laid Your life down just for me,
And even called me friend.

Your love is so overwhelming,
In your presence it is hard to stand,
You stilled the storm within my heart,
Now my life is in Your hand.

There is no-one like You, Jesus,
You are everything to me,
You raised me up to be your servant,
You opened my eyes to see.

You have given me a second chance,
A life blessed by Your love,
To declare Your praises to all I meet,
My hope comes from above.

Until that day comes passing by,
And the Son comes for His bride,
I will put my hand to doing Your will,
Putting all my burdens aside.

You have been so Gracious to me,
Your mercy never seems to cease,
My aim in life is to bring You praise,
And walk with You in Your peace.

I thank you that You died for me,
You took my sin and shame,
Nailing it all to that wooden cross,
So that I would bear Your name.

I never realised the treasure I had,
Buried deep within my heart,
Until the Spirit from above,
Gave me a brand new start.

I no longer live as satan's fool,
That's how I used to live,
God's Spirit taught me how to love,
And how I should forgive.

Reflecting on the life I once lived,
I now can plainly see,
There were moments in my past, sad life,
That You were watching over me.

I am so eternally grateful,
For the sacrifice you gave,
I now walk with the King of Kings,
Only He has the power to save.

Now I am empowered by Your Spirit,
And cleansed by YOUR shed blood,
I walk by faith in You, my Lord,
Your favour comes like a flood.

I stand before You, humbly,
Confessing all my sin,
I thank You for Your mercy,
I am renewed from within.

You have been so Gracious to me,
You are the Father's Son,
My life is Yours, please have Your way,
Thank you Lord, for all You've done,

Written and Edited, 10/12/2010,
By David T. Gilbert.

PARKINSON'S PAIN

Parkinson's Disease is
a very cruel curse,
It's victims are randomly sought,
Age is no barrier,
nor gender or race,
It's the toughest battle to be fought.

At first, you seem unbalanced,
And your steps get shorter,
Your speech starts to change and slur,
You can't write as you should,
And you shuffle about,
Normal function seems harder to endure.

The drugs you need,
Only you can use,
The time for each dose is precise,
At the start,
Late doses have little effect,
But as time goes by, you'll think twice.

You will feel in your body,

As each month goes by,

Your weight seems to be heading down,

Aches and pains slowly appear,

Increasing each time,

People notice, and start to frown.

Not a soul understands,

What it means to us,

Each case differs from the rest,

There are no two cases,

Exactly the same,

It is like an endurance test.

Sexual activity,

That's the first to go,

Then muscle fat slowly decreases,

In your arms, you feel weaker,

And gets harder to live,

It's the most challenging of all life's diseases.

As each Winter goes by,

The cold gets more intense,

Your legs and feet freeze without warning,

Movement is a no go,

Till you warm up again,

It's quite a task to arise each morning.

As your medication is increased,
And your body wears out,
You start thinking of the worst,
You question the time,
That you have to live freely,
You wonder why it's you that seems cursed.

Your feet start to tangle,
It gets harder just to stand,
You seem to fall without reason,
Your muscles uncontrollably
Twist and spasm,
Your independence finally ends it's season.

You need the assistance
Of family members,
Even for the simplest of tasks,
You feel so embarrassed,
To request their help,
Wishing that the day would pass.

You think of the times,
When you would work all day,
Earning good money to feed your kin,
Enduring long hours,
At times, without rest,
Those days, you enjoyed to the end.

But now it seems
Those days are gone,
They remain as passed memories,
You thank the Lord,
For each day you're alive,
And make the most of your opportunities.

Each day I wake,
I give thanks to my God,
For the honour of bearing His Name,
"I must stay positive',
I say to myself,
I don't want my life ending in shame.

If I thought too much,
About my afflicted life,
I would probably prefer to die,
But God is my Hope,
My Rock and my Strength,
But still, there is the question, 'WHY?'.

I have learned that
Life is like that,
It catches you by surprise,
We live in a world,
That is dying from sin,
Many things will open your eyes.

This disease is non selective,
No matter who you are,
We all are equal to God,
It's only our faith
That gives us an edge,
Thank you Father, for Your Holy Word.

So next time you see,
A person as described,
Like the one in this long poem,
Maybe you will consider
The plight they are in,
And try to help with their problem.

It's not your sympathy
We are crying out for,
Nor having a shoulder when all gets demanding,
We need your support
When times get tough,
And a lot of understanding.

David T. Gilbert.

Written and Edited by David T. Gilbert,
15/12/2010.

PARKINSON'S NOTE

You may think I'm odd, with the way I walk,

it may seem hard to understand, my unusual talk,

my staggering about, may cause you confusion,

my movements and actions seem like an illusion,

it isn't that I'm drunk, or as high as a kite,

it may embarrass you, to know my sad plight,

But, be at peace, mate, take it steady, and be at ease,

I need a little slack, 'cause I have PARKINSON'S DISEASE!

Written and Edited 11/12/2010, by David T. Gilbert.

SAFE IN THE ARMS OF JESUS

It's such a wonderful joy to know,

I'm safe in the arms of Jesus,

While the world is falling apart all around,

Only His presence is what really pleases,

The world is full of confusion and doubt,

not knowing what tomorrow brings,

But Jesus fills my life with hope,

He cares for the smallest of things,

I stand so secure by His Grace and love,

His promises are genuine and true,

He brings joy to my soul and peace to my heart,

each morning, His mercies are new,

There are times in my life, when I've got it wrong,

and have failed to shine for His Glory,

But He wants me to live one day at a time,

but I guess that's another story,

He wants us to believe in His love,

even though we feel unworthy,

And accept His gift of eternal life,

and change from being worldly,

There's nothing you can do to turn His love,

He remains faithful to the end,

You won't find anyone who will love you more,

Or will be a closer friend.

Written and Edited, 25/06/2012, by David T. Gilbert.

TO BE MORE LIKE JESUS

To be more like the Lord Jesus, should be our aim in life,

Following His example, and avoiding any strife.

Like looking into a mirror, and reflecting His Glory,

Telling the whole world, of His salvation story.

He came to this humble earth, from Heaven up above,

At Calvary He died for man, revealing His undying love.

While we were still lost in sin, He obediently went to the cross,

It was us who gained salvation, it was Heaven that finally lost.

The grave had no power at all, to hold our Saviour down,

Now to all who believe in Him, there awaits a golden crown.

The victory that He won that day, was given over to us,

Now we are seated in heaven with Him, in His name, we are victorious,

THE GRACE OF GOD

The Grace of God is amazing, too great to comprehend,
We fail to fully understand, God's desire to be our friend.
He paid the price for all our sin, by His stripes, we have been healed,
He purchased us to be His own, He is our strength and shield.
If only we would take the time, to hearken to His voice,
He's not the type to force His will, He's given us a free will choice,
But most of us just rush around, in our own precarious way,
Hardly ever stopping to notice, or taking time to pray,
When trouble rears its ugly head, we quickly run and hide,
Without ever knowing the peace, of Jesus by your side.
He cares about the little things, that cause us worry and fret,
If only we would trust in Him, our lives would be free of regret.
He patiently waits till we are done, and finally we are through,
Then we realise its by His grace, we live our lives anew,
We run our race in such a way, as to win the prize,
Our reward is at the finish line, if only we would open our eyes.
It's by God's grace we worship Him, lifting up His only Son,
And establish a sure relationship, with God's Holy One.

Written & Edited by David T. Gilbert, 30/04/2012.
Word count – 236, A4 pages = 1.

POETRY IS . . .

Poetry to me, is very unique,
A somewhat creative form of art,
Having a romance of it's very own,
It is written straight from the heart.

It is an expression of the poet's own self,
Reflecting His character and his gift,
It should never degrade, insult or tear down,
But always encourage and uplift.

Poetry should make you feel great,
When all around seems bad,
A word to brighten up your day,
Without you feeling too sad.

It tugs at your very heart inside,
Captivating your deepest emotions,
Relating to the stories it tells,
Identifying with the poet's notions.

Poetry, to me, should be simple to read,
Not weighed down with modern day yack,
The story line should be one to enjoy,
From the front cover to the back.

poetry should hold your interest,
And grab you passionately,
Like a love letter written to your wife,
On your 30th wedding Anniversary.

Practical applications,
Of the point it puts across,
Should be the order of the day,
So no important point is lost.

Poetry is also creative,
You may write about any idea,
The limits you reach for are without end,
Inspiring faith instead of fear.

Poetry is as creative,
As any art can be,
To write a poem that grabs you,
And opens your eyes to see.

Drawing ideas from deep inside,
Treasures of silver and gold,
Is a gift from God, a talent so rare,
Bringing up precious stories to be told.

Poetry should be a means to think,
To reflect on days gone by.
Of memories of happiness, peace and joy,
And friendships that make you cry.

So now you have an idea,
of my passion and desire,
To be able to reach both young and old,
And spreading the Spirit's fire.

I trust that as you read my work,
You are blessed in every way,
My gift comes from my God above,
May God bless you all each day.

David T. Gilbert.

Written and Edited, 10/`12/2010, by David T. Gilbert.

MY BESSIEMAE

What could be said of my BessieMae, my Companion, Best Friend, my
Wife,
She entered my life like a cool summer breeze, giving me a fresh start at life.

Her heart is full of wisdom, she has a very deep love,
Her faithfulness is always noted by the God of Heaven above.

She is like a pirates Treasure Chest, overflowing with Silver and Gold,
Each day she reveals hidden Treasures, buried deep within her soul.

She seems to have an insight that no-one else can see,
Revealing things only the Spirit would know, she always fascinated me.

BessieMae was everything I ever wanted, but I thought I could never
behold,
She taught me so much about life and love, she truly is a treasure of
Gold.

I had nothing to offer when I first met my love, I had wasted my life away,
But she led me to my Lord and King, and now, we share each day.

Our union has lasted now for 30 years, without a single regret,
I still reflect with tears of great joy, the very day that we met.

I am so in love with this Treasure from God, she is surely a gift from above,
I pray that we are a pleasant example, of God's unfathomable Love,

HAPPY WEDDING ANNIVERSARY,
MY BESSIEMAE.

From your loving Husband, David T. Gilbert. 22/11/2010

WHAT IS A CHAMPION?

What is a champion, you may very well ask?
What makes a man seem to just stand out?
To be very different from just one of the crowd,
To be respected as a leader, by those all about.

In the Bible, the list of champions are many,
It stretches from Genesis to Revelation,
Doing exploits and mighty deeds for God,
In every land and every nation.

Men like Abraham, Joshua and Caleb,
Gideon, Nehemiah, Samson too,
Isaac, Jacob, David, Solomon,
They were examples for me and you.

Like David, who faced Goliath,
This bloke was nine feet tall,
But Goliath had confidence in his size,
David trusted in the God of all.

Shadrach, Meshach, and Abednego,
Their story inspires great faith,
They refused to honour the King's idol,
Finding favour by way of God's grace.

Elijah, Elishah, Samuel and Job,
Too many to try and mention,
Put their trust and faith in God above,
Looking to God for divine intervention.

But, in the Bible's New Testament,
A different type of champion arises,
One who will turn the other cheek,
And who's conduct and attitude surprises.

The New Testament looks at life itself,
Giving instruction on how to live,
Instead of being selfish and full of pride,
We are commanded to love and forgive.

We are to be Holy before our God,
For sin has no place in our lives,
We are also to be obedient to our God,
And walk in the ways of the Wise.

To reflect the attributes of our King,
Obeying Him without question,
Is not just a mild request from above,
Or even a hopeful suggestion.

The Fruit of the Spirit is evidence enough,
Of the indwelling God above,
The way of the world is evil and false,
But, God's way is Mercy and Love.

It takes a lot of courage and faith,
To make a stand for our Lord,
Facing ridicule, humiliation and shame,
Being bold, declaring His Word.

Our calling is to make disciples of men,
Telling them that Jesus lives,
Displaying a better way of life,
The Glory is ever His.

Missionaries have suffered martyrdom,
In the cruellest possible way,
They would rather face death than deny their God,
Looking forward to a better day.

Jesus is our prime example,
When it comes to pleasing the Lord,
He took over three years to teach us all,
Being obedient to God's Word.

He taught us about God's Holy law,
About forgiveness and about love,
He also told us what it would cost,
To be forever with God above.

He showed us all the Father's heart,
Despite the Pharisee's contention,
He stood for the truth, facing them head-on,
Trusting in the Father's intervention.

To judge Him guilty on a pack of lies,
They had to break their own law,
They treated Him like a sheep among wolves,
They cursed Him, and they swore.

But even then, He never complained,
Instead, He chose to forgive,
Setting us a pure example,
Of how we should really live.

When we respond to His Salvation call,
We become a Champion for God,
Being cleansed from sin by the Blood of Christ,
And daily reading God's word.

Your heavenly Father loves you all,
He calls to 'whosoever will,'
Come, drink from the River of Life, freely,
Come all, and have your fill.

I once had lived a sinner's life,
Pleasing no one but me alone,
But then, when I met Jesus Christ,
He called me one of His own.

I have been a Champion for Jesus now,
Working faithfully for my Saviour,
I love encouraging other people,
Knowing that I have God's favour.

So, in light of what has been written,
And what you know to be true,
Do you think you are a Champion,
Because I know I am one, too!

Written & edited by David T. Gilbert, 28/11/2010.

'JESSICA'

Jessica, your smile brings joy to my heart,

You are such an encouragement, right from the start.

You greet me with the highest honor and respect,

The kindness of Jesus, is what you reflect.

I love and honor you. above all else,

My prayer is to bless you, with life and good health.

I pray you are blessed abundantly,

In life and in love, eternally.

You will always have a special place in my heart,

To me, you're a Champion, and a work of art.

In all that you do, success follows you,

Your presence is as fresh as the morning dew.

The favor of God is with you in life,

Blessed is the man who makes you his wife.

Written and Edited, 4/11/2011, by David T. Gilbert.

TO MY FRIEND & SPIRITUAL FATHER;

Though many years have passed us by,
My honour of you will never die,

In my opinion, you would have to be,
A man of the highest Integrity,

Your example is unique, rarely seen these days,
It is men like you who teach us good ways,

You humbly walk with God each morn,
And encourage all from dusk till dawn,

You never get upset with fits of rages,
You always trust in The ROCK of AGES,

Your children rejoice, your Grandchildren too,
They love you completely, just for being You,

I have been highly honoured, from way back then,
For knowing you as a Father & friend.

With the Highest Honour & Respect,
David T. Gilbert.

GOD IS ON THE THRONE

No matter what we face in life, God is on the Throne,

Regardless of trouble, turmoil or strife, He shields His very own.

The eyes of the Lord are in every place, beholding the things that we do,

He is a shield to His righteous ones, each morn, His mercies are new.

Our God is known as the Ancient of Days, He lives eternally,

Opening the eyes of the spiritually blind, so that they can plainly see.

All creation is subject to our God, He is the Omnipotent Lord,

Creator of all things that are seen, according to His Word.

We are His chosen people, protected by His love,

Having faith in His only Son, who came down from above.

He showed us how to live for Him, and how to simply forgive,

He died upon a wooden cross, now it's for Him that we live.

One day He'll come back for His Bride, of which I am a part,

That's the day we all go home, I know it in my heart.

Written & Edited, 30/04/2012, by David T. Gilbert.

JUST A WHISPER AWAY

God is just a whisper away, He's much closer than you think,

He knows what brings joy to our hearts, and what drives us to the brink.

He knows the things that worry us, He knows what brings us peace,

He understands when we have fear, and what brings us release.

His love was there when we were born, and when we went to School,

As we went through our childhood days, and thought life was so cool.

God was there when we reached adulthood, and bought our first neat car,

The day we met our future wife, and observed the morning star.

He was there when we needed a loving friend, when all life fell apart,

When we needed someone to set us straight, and spoke right from the heart.

God was there when we shed our first tear, and watched us cry in pain,

When we thought we weren't good enough, making blunders time and again.

God is near you every day, just waiting for the right season,

When you will turn to acknowledge Him, and humbly see He's the reason.

He went to the cross at Calvary, to set us free from sin,

And now, due to our faith in Christ, we are reborn from within.

He lived to teach us Heaven's ways, and died to show His love,

He walked this troubled earth for us, and sent His Snow White Dove.

He wants our hearts of obedience, and to be as pure as He,

We are a people chosen by God, in Christ, we are set free.

So if you think that no-one cares, and that you stand alone,

Remember who is Lord of All, and who sits on the Throne.

We need to cast our cares on Him, because He cares for us,

He paid for sin with His own blood, His grace is amazing enough.

God loves you more than you could ever know, just turn to Him today,

He will hold you close in arms of love, and direct your every way.

Written & Edited 2/05/2012, by David T. Gilbert.

WHAT IF . . .

One day, I sat and asked myself,
What if there was no God?
No hope of any future above,
No Holy written Word.
What would we be really living for?
Our days wouldn't really matter,
We'd have no purpose to our lives,
We'd simply run and scatter.
There would be no sense in learning,
No use for technology,
Why would we live to improve our lives?
Or follow set laws and decrees.
And what about morality,
What need would there to be Holy?
Like the animals that run free and wild,
How depressing it would be.
What idol would we worship?
If there were any at all?
Would we still need a saviour,
To stop us from a fall?
Would anyone care about our lives?
Would there be a need for love?
Life would be dull and drab to me,
If there was no God above!
But I know that there is a God,

Who showed His love for me,

He died upon a splintery cross,

Just to set me free.

I live by His amazing grace,

I belong to Jesus Christ!

Living as He had planned for me,

He's the lover of my life.

Written and Edited, 24/01/012, by David T. Gilbert.

WHO REALLY IS TO BLAME?

Who really is to blame,
For our troubles and our woes?
We tend to blame others,
As the old saying goes.
But we tend to forget,
We are given a choice,
To listen to the lie,
Or hearken to God's voice.
Yes, Eve did take the fruit,
As recorded in God's Word,
Because of her actions,
We lost intimacy with the Lord.
But Adam was made head,
God put him in charge,
But he blamed Eve,
It was her fault, by and large.
It's easy, to point the finger,
Finding other folk to blame,
But we can never avoid the fact,
It's our sin and shame.
Whatever you focus on,
Will come out in your life,
Your confession is important,
When avoiding strife.

The examples that we follow,

Have an impact on how we live,

We can choose to live for pleasure,

Or choose to lovingly forgive.

We need to be accountable,

For the way we live our life,

Each action done, each word confessed,

Some choices end in strife.

The devil is our accuser,

He's a liar, and a thief,

His mission is to destroy,

He's a threat to your belief.

He entices with temptation,

He's relentless with his attack,

But don't ever give up,

That's just like turning back.

His mission is to keep us,

From intimacy with the Lord,

He will throw you off track,

And stop you from God's Word.

But greater is He who is in you,

Than he who is in the earth,

The empty tomb proves who won,

We are saved by God's re-birth.

But, although he is our accuser,

We still have to choose,

How will you decide to live today,

To win, or to lose?

Be wise and alert in your walk,

Not as foolish, but as wise,

Be aware of our enemy's tricks,

Make sure you open your eyes.

The only power that he has,

Is the ability to deceive,

So do not believe in lies,

Trust Jesus, and receive.

Jesus is the only way,

To escape this troubled life,

By accepting Him as your King,

You avoid much trouble and strife.

Satan's world is full of hate,

You'll have no friends in there,

But Jesus loves you endlessly,

You'll find, He really does care.

Written and Edited, 6/05/2012, by David T. Gilbert.

GOD'S WORD

Each time I look into God's Word, I cannot help but see,

An eternal God of loving Grace, who died to set me free.

He had in mind who would be saved, before He created the earth,

He chose me just to be with Him, by way of His plan of re-birth.

Before I ever knew who He was, or had faith in His name,

He died upon that splintery cross, to pay for my sin and shame.

While I was full of hate and sin, and blatant arrogant pride,

He stood beside me patiently, watching by my side.

The days when I would act the fool, just to have a friend,

Would grieve the Holy Spirit quite oft, but I lost in the end.

What is written in the Word of God, is truth in its purest form,

Filled with wisdom and garnished with love, a rock amid the storm.

Our God is an eternal God, omnipotent and mighty is He,

He sits upon the thunderclouds, and rides the stormy sea.

He laughs at the folly of mankind, He is wisest of them all,

He is a shield to His faithful ones, and saves them from a fall.

He cares about the little things, that matter only to me,

He helps me to be everything, He created me to be.

He wants His children to trust Him, He's faithful to His promise,

He shows His love to all mankind, bestowing His Grace upon us.

So if you think God isn't for you, or you don't make the grade,

We are all human by design, we stumble time and again.

We need a Saviour to rescue us, someone who understands,
Who has been through life with all it's woes, and still has clean pure hands.
We cannot make it by ourselves, we need God's Word of Truth,
Jesus is the only way, He is God's living proof.

Written and Edited, 31/05/2012, by David T. Gilbert.

THE CROSSROADS OF LIFE

The crossroads of life, are really our choice,
An opportunity to hearken, to the Lords voice,
We have been Divinely given, the sole right to choose,
Whether we win, or whether we lose,
Jesus, our Lord, is the only sure way,
We are born again, by faith in His Name,
Even if you think, your life is a mess,
It's our choice to live, by what we confess.
Jesus came to this earth, to teach us God's ways,
To pay for our sin, and lengthen our days,
He spoke about peace, and the need to forgive,
Because of His death, we are now free to live.
We are called to be Holy, in all that we do,
Reflecting His Glory, and living life anew.
If people don't see, the Jesus we preach,
How can we claim, to know who we teach.
It's all about Jesus, who called us to be,
Ambassadors for Him, reflecting His Glory.
The choice is our choice, to believe Him or not,
If you don't fancy heaven, the alternative is HOT.

Written & Edited, 6/05/2012, by David T. Gilbert.

IF WE COULD ALL GO BACK IN TIME

If we could all go back in time,
And correct the mistakes of our past,
Reliving our lives till we got it right,
Would it be an impossible task?
Would you return to your early childhood,
Or maybe those early school years,
Maybe you'd return to your very first job,
Reliving the past with fears.
Or maybe to one time long ago,
when you really lost your cool,
Acting in such an irate, rash way,
It made you look the fool.
Maybe you would return to your wedding day,
Or when you had your first child,
But no matter what moment you revisited your past,
Would your life be so peaceful and mild.
How many times would you need to live,
Just to get one blunder right,
None of us are perfect, or exact,
Or blameless in God's Holy sight.
We often look for someone to blame,
For the trouble that comes our way,
When we are the ones responsible,
For the trouble and games we play.

We need to appreciate the life we live,

Accepting the good with the bad,

Taking account of our shame and regret,

For the unfortunate moments we had.

Our past mistakes shape our character in life,

Making us who we are,

You can't surprise God, He knows all things,

Using wisdom will help you go far.

The lives we live, and the choices we make,

Everything in life that we do,

These must be seen in a positive light,

Building character in me and you.

Life is what you make of it,

We only get one chance at best,

So do your best by leaving your mark,

Let the Spirit do the rest.

Written and Edited, 23/02/2012, by David T. Gilbert.